Contents

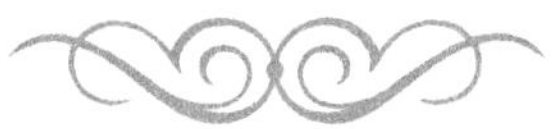

1. Any Person May Become Great 7
2. Heredity and Opportunity 12
3. The Source of Power 16
4. The Mind of God 20
5. Preparation 24
6. The Social Point of View 27
7. The Individual Point of View 32
8. Consecration 35
9. Identification 39
10. Idealization 42
11. Realization 46
12. Hurry and Habit 50
13. Thought 54

14. Action at Home 58
15. Action Abroad 62
16. Some Further Explanations 67
17. More about Thought 71
18. Jesus' Idea of Greatness 76
19. A View of Evolution 80
20. Serving God 85
21. A Mental Exercise 90

BESTSELLING NON-FICTION

BESTSELLING NON-FICTION

- Relativity by Albert Einstein
  Science/Physics, ISBN: 9789380914220
- Reminiscences of a Stock Operator by Edwin Lefevre
  Business/Stock Market, ISBN: 9788194764816
- Success Through a Positive Mental Attitude by Napoleon Hill
  Self-Help, ISBN: 9789390492435
- The Art of War by Sun Tzu
  Self-Help, ISBN: 9789380914893
- The Autobiography of a Yogi by Paramahansa Yogananda
  Biographies & Memoirs, ISBN: 9789380914602
- The Diary of a Young Girl by Anne Frank
  Biographies & Memoirs, ISBN: 9789380914312
- The Elements of Style by William Strunk
  Non-Fiction, ISBN: 9789389157123
- The Law of Success by Napoleon Hill
  Self-Help, ISBN: 9788180320927
- The Power of Your Subconscious Mind by Joseph Murphy
  Self-Help, ISBN: 9788180320958
- The Richest Man in Babylon by George S. Clason
  Business & Economics, ISBN: 9789387669369
- The Science of Getting Rich by Wallace D. Wattles
  Self-Help, ISBN: 9788180320972
- The World as I See It by Albert Einstein
  Non-Fiction, ISBN: 9789388118125

Search the book by its ISBN

THE SCIENCE OF BEING GREAT

Wallace D. Wattles

GENERAL PRESS

Published by

GENERAL PRESS

4805/24, Fourth Floor, Krishna House
Ansari Road, Daryaganj, New Delhi - 110002
Ph : 011-23282971, 45795759
E-mail : generalpressindia@gmail.com

www.generalpress.in

First Edition : 2022

ISBN : 9789354993886

Published by Azeem Ahmad Khan for General Press

Chapter 1

Any Person May Become Great

There is a Principle of Power in every person. By the intelligent use and direction of this principle, man can develop his own mental faculties. Man has an inherent power by which he may grow in whatsoever direction he pleases, and there does not appear to be any limit to the possibilities of his growth. No man has yet become so great in any faculty but that it is possible for someone else to become greater. The possibility is in the Original Substance from which man is made. Genius is Omniscience flowing into man.

Genius is more than talent. Talent may merely be one faculty developed out of proportion to other faculties, but genius is the union of man and God in the acts of the soul. Great men are always greater than their deeds. They are in connection with a reserve power that is without limit. We do not know where the boundary of the mental powers of man is; we do not even know that there is a boundary.

The power of conscious growth is not given to the lower animals; it is mans alone and may he developed and increased by him. The lower animals can, to a great extent, be trained and developed by man; but man can train and develop himself. He alone has this power, and he has it to an apparently unlimited extent.

The purpose of life for man is growth, just as the purpose of life for trees and plants is growth. Trees and plains grow automatically and along fixed lines; man can grow as he will. Trees and plants can only develop certain possibilities and characteristics; man can develop any power which is or has been shown by any person, anywhere. Nothing that is possible in spirit is impossible in flesh and blood. Nothing that man can think is impossible in action. Nothing that man can imagine is impossible of realization.

Man is formed for growth, and he is under the necessity of growing.

It is essential to his happiness that he should continuously advance.

Life without progress becomes unendurable, and the person who ceases from growth must either become imbecile or insane. The greater and more harmonious and well-rounded his growth, the happier man will be.

There is no possibility in any man that is not in every man: but if they proceed naturally, no two men will grow into the same thing, or he alike. Every man comes into the world with a predisposition to grow along certain lines, and growth is easier for him along those lines than in any other way. This is a wise provision, for it gives endless variety. It is as if a gardener should throw all his bulbs into one basket; to the superficial observer they would look alike, but growth reveals a tremendous difference. So of men and women: they are like the basket of bulbs. One may be a rose and add brightness and color to sonic dark corner of the world; one may be a lily and teach a lesson of love and purity to every eye that sees; one may be a climbing vine and hide the rugged outlines of some dark rock; one may be a great oak among whose boughs the birds shall nest and sing, and beneath whose shade the docks shall rest at noon, but everyone will be something worthwhile. Something rare, something perfect.

There are undreamed of possibilities in the common lives all around us; in a large sense, there are no "common" people. In times of national stress and peril the cracker-box loafer of the corner store and the village drunkard become heroes and statesmen through the quickening of the Principle of Power within them. There is a genius in every man and woman, waiting to be brought forth. Every village has its great man or woman; someone to whom all go for advice in time of trouble; someone who is instinctively recognized as being great in wisdom and insight. To such a one the minds of the whole community turn in times of local crisis; he is tacitly recognized as being great. He does small thing in a great way. He could do great things as well if he did but undertake them; so can any man; so can you. The Principle of Power gives us just what we ask of it; if we only undertake little things, it only gives us power for little things; but if we try to do great things in a great way it gives us all the power there is.

But beware of undertaking great things in a small way; of that we shall speak farther on.

There are two mental attitudes a man may take. One makes him like a football. It has resilience and reacts strongly when force is applied to it, but it originates nothing; it never acts of itself. There is no power within it. Men of this type are controlled by circumstances and environment; their destinies are decided by things external to themselves. The Principle of Power within them is never really active at all. They never speak or act from within. The other attitude makes man like a flowing spring. Power comes out from the center of him. He has within him a well of water springing up into everlasting life. He radiates force; he is felt by his environment. The Principle of Power in him is in constant action. He is self-active. "He hath life in himself."

No greater good can come to any man or woman than to become self-active. All the experiences of life are designed by Providence to force men and women into self-activity; to compel them to cease being creatures of circumstances and master their environment. In his lowest stage, man is the child of chance and circumstance and the slave of tear. His acts are all reactions resulting from the impingement upon him of forces in his environment. He acts only as he is acted upon; he originates nothing. But the lowest savage has within him a Principle of Power sufficient to master all that he fears and if he learns this and becomes self-active, he becomes as one of the gods.

The awakening of the Principle of Power in man is the real conversion; the passing from death to life. It is when the dead hear the voice of the Son of Man and come forth and live. It is the resurrection and the life. When it is awakened, man becomes a son of the Highest and all power is given to him in heaven and on earth.

Nothing was ever in any man that is not in you; no man ever had more spiritual or mental power than you can attain, or did greater things than you can accomplish. You can become what you want to be.

Chapter 2

Heredity and Opportunity

You are not barred front attaining greatness by heredity. No matter who or what your ancestors may have been or how unlearned or lowly their station, the upward way is open for you. There is no such thing as inheriting a fixed mental position; no matter how small the mental capital we receive from our parents, it may be increased; no man is born incapable of growth.

Heredity counts for something. We are born with subconscious mental tendencies; as, for instance, a tendency to melancholy, or cowardice, or to ill-temper; but all these subconscious tendencies may be overcome. When the real man awakens and comes forth he can throw them off very easily. Nothing of this kind need keep you down; if you have inherited undesirable mental tendencies, you can eliminate them and put desirable tendencies in their places. An inherited mental trait is a habit of thought of your father or mother impressed upon your subconscious mind: you can substitute the opposite impression by forming the opposite habit of thought. You can substitute a habit of cheerfulness for a tendency to despondency: you can overcome cowardice or ill-temper.

Heredity may count for something, too, in an inherited conformation of the skull. There is something in phrenology. If not so much as its exponents claim for it: it is true that the different faculties are localized in the brain, and that the power of a faculty depends upon the number of active brain cells in its area. A faculty whose brain area is large is likely to act with more power than one whose cranial section is small; hence persons with certain conformations of the skull show talent as musicians, orators, mechanics, and so on. It has been argued from this that a man's cranial formation must, to a great extent, decide his station in life, but this is an error. It has been found that a small brain section, with many fine and active cells, gives as powerful expression to faculty as a larger brain with coarser cells; and it has been found that by turning the Principle of Power into any section of the brain, with the will And purpose to develop a particular talent, the brain cells may be multi plied indefinitely. Any faculty, power, or talent you possess, no matter how small or rudimentary, may be increased; you can multiply the brain cells in this particular area until it acts as powerfully as you wish. It is true that you can act most easily through those faculties that are now most largely developed; you can do, with the least effort, the things which "come naturally"; but it is also true that if you will make the necessary effort you can develop any talent. You can do what you desire to do and become what you want to be. When you fix upon some ideal and proceed as hereinafter directed, all the power of your being is turned into the faculties required in the realization of that ideal; more blood and nerve three go to the corresponding sections of the brain, and the cells are quickened, increased, and multiplied in number. The proper use of the mind of man will build a brain capable of doing what the mind wants to do.

The brain does not make the man; the man makes the brain.

Your place in life is not fixed by heredity.

Nor are you condemned to the lower levels by circumstances or lack of opportunity. The Principle of Power in man is sufficient for all the requirements of his soul. No possible combination of circumstances can keep him down, if he makes his personal attitude right and determines to rise. The power which formed man and purposed him for growth also controls the circumstances of society, industry, and government; and this power is never divided against itself. The power which is in you is in the things around you, and when you begin to move forward, the things will arrange themselves for your advantage, as described in later chapters of this book. Man was formed for growth, and all things external were designed to promote his growth. No sooner does a man awaken his soul and enter on the advancing way than he finds that not only is God for him, but nature, society, and his fellow man are for him also; and all things work together for his good if he obeys the law. Poverty is no bar to greatness, for poverty can always be removed. Martin Luther, as a child, sang in the streets for bread. Linnaeus the naturalist had only forty dollars with which to educate himself; he mended his own shoes and often had to beg meals from his friends. Hugh Miller, apprentice to a stone mason, began to study geology in a quarry, George Stephenson, inventor or the locomotive engine, and one of the greatest of civil engineers, was coal miner, working in mine, when he awakened and began to think. James Watt was a sickly child, and was not strong enough to be sent to school. Abraham Lincoln was a poor boy. In each of these cases we see a Principle of Power in the man which lifts him above all opposition and adversity.

There is a Principle of Power in you if you use it and apply it in a certain way you can overcome all heredity, and master all circumstances and conditions and become a great and powerful personality.

Chapter 3

The Source of Power

Man's brain, body, mind, faculties, and talents are the mere instruments he uses in demonstrating greatness; in themselves they do not make him great. A maim may have a large brain and a good mind, strong faculties, and brilliant talents, and yet he is not a great man unless he uses all these in a great way. That quality which enables man to use his abilities in a great way makes him great; and to that quality we give the name of wisdom. Wisdom is the essential basis of greatness.

Wisdom is the power to perceive the best ends to aim at and the best means for reaching those ends. It is the power to perceive the right thing to do. The man who is wise enough to know the right thing to do, who is good enough to wish to do only the right thing, and who is able and strong enough to do the right thing is a truly great man. He will instantly become marked as a personality of power in any community and men will delight to do him honor.

Wisdom is dependent upon knowledge. Where there is complete ignorance there can be no wisdom, no knowledge of the right thing to do. Man's knowledge is comparatively limited and so his wisdom must be small, unless he can connect his mind with a knowledge greater than his own and draw front it, by inspiration, the wisdom that his own limitations deny him. This he can do; this is what the really great men and women have done. Man's knowledge is limited and uncertain; therefore he caning have wisdom in himself.

Only God knows all truth: therefore only God can have real wisdom or know the right thing to do at all times, and man can receive wisdom from God. I proceed to give an illustration: Abraham Lincoln had limited education; but he had the power to perceive truth. In Lincoln we see pre-eminently apparent the fact that real wisdom consists in knowing the right thing to do at all times and under all circumstances; in having the will to do the right thing, and in I raving talent and ability enough to be competent and able to do the right thing.

Back in the days of the abolition agitation, and during the compromise period, when all other men were more or less confused as to what was right or as to what ought to be done. Lincoln was never uncertain. He saw through the superficial arguments of the pro slavery men; he saw, also, the impracticability and fanaticism of the abolitionists; he saw the right ends to aim at and he saw the best means to attain those ends. It was because men recognized that he perceived truth and knew the right thing to do that they made him president. Any man who develops the power to perceive truth, and who can show that he always knows the right thing to do and that he can be trusted to do the right thing, will he honored and advanced; the whole world is looking eagerly for such men.

When Lincoln became president he was surrounded by a multitude of so-called able advisers, hardly any two of whom were agreed. At times they were all opposed to his policies; at times almost the whole North was opposed to what he proposed to do. But he saw the truth when others were misled by appearances: his judgment was seldom or never wrong. He was at once the ablest statesman and the best soldier of the period.

Where did he, a comparatively unlearned man, get this wisdom? It was not due to some peculiar formation of his skull or to sonic fineness of texture of his brain. It was not due to sonic physical characteristic. It was not even a quality of mind due to superior reasoning power. Knowledge of truth is not often reached by the processes of reason. It was due to a spiritual insight. He perceived truth, but where did he perceive it and whence did the perception come? We see something similar in Washington, whose faith and courage, due to his perception of truth, held the colonies together during the long and often apparently hopeless struggle of the Revolution. We see something of the same thing in the phenomenal genius of Napoleon, who always knew, in military matters, the best means to adopt. We see that the greatness of Napoleon was in nature rather than in Napoleon, and we discover back of Washington and Lincoln something greater than either Washington or Lincoln. We see the same thing in all great men and women.

They perceive truth; but truth cannot be perceived until it exists; and there can be no truth until there is a mind to perceive it. Truth does not exist apart from mind. Washington and Lincoln were in touch and communication with a mind which knew all knowledge and contained all truth. So of all who manifest wisdom.

Wisdom is obtained by reading the mind of God.

Chapter 4

The Mind of God

There is a Cosmic Intelligence which is in all things and through all things. This is the one real substance. From it all things proceed. It is Intelligent Substance or Mind Stuff. It is God.

Where there is no substance there can be no intelligence; for where there is no substance there is nothing. Where there is thought there must be a substance which thinks. Thought cannot be function, for function is motion, and it is inconceivable that mere motion should think. Thought cannot be vibration, for vibration is motion, and that motion should be intelligent is not thinkable. Motion is nothing but the moving of substance; if there be intelligence shown it must be in the substance and not in the motion. Thought cannot be the result of motions in the brain; if thought is in the brain it must be in the brain's substance and not in the motions which brain substance makes.

But thought is not in the brain substance, for brain substance, without life, is quite unintelligent and dead. Thought is in the life-principle which animates the brain; in the spirit substance, which is the real man. The brain does not think, the man thinks and expresses his thought through the brain.

There is a spirit substance which thinks. Just as the spirit substance of man permeates his body, and thinks and knows in the body, so the Original Spirit Substance, God, permeates all nature and thinks and knows in nature. Nature is as intelligent as man, and knows more than man; nature knows all things. The All-Mind has been in touch with all things from the beginning: and it contains all knowledge. Man's experience covers a few things, and these things man knows; but God's experience covers all the things that have happened since the creation, from the wreck of a planet or the passing of a comet to the fall of a sparrow. All that is and all that has been are present in the Intelligence which is wrapped about us and enfolds us and presses upon us from every side.

All the encyclopedias men have written are but trivial affairs compared to the vast knowledge held by the mind in which men live, move, and have their being.

The truths men perceive by inspiration are thoughts held in this mind. If they were not thoughts men could not perceive them, for they would have no existence; and they could not exist as thoughts unless there is a mind for them to exist in; and a mind can be nothing else than a substance which thinks.

Man is thinking substance, a portion of the Cosmic Substance; but man is limited, while the Cosmic Intelligence from which be sprang, which Jesus calls the Father, is unlimited. All intelligence, power, and force come from the Father. Jesus recognized this and stated it very plainly. Over and over again he ascribed all his wisdom and power to his unity with the Father, and to his perceiving the thoughts of God. "My Father and I are one." This was the foundation of his knowledge and power. He showed the people the necessity of becoming spiritually awakened; of hearing his voice and becoming like him. He compared the unthinking man who is the prey and sport of circumstances to the dead man in a tomb, and besought him to hear and come forth. "God is Spirit." he said; "be born again, become spiritually awake, and you may see His kingdom. Hear my voice; see what I am and what I do, and come forth and live. The words I speak are spirit and life; accept them and they will cause a well of water to spring up within you. Then you will have life within yourself."

"I do what I see the Father do;" he said, meaning that he read the thoughts of God. "The Father showeth all things to the Son." "If any man has the will to do the will of God, he shall know truth: "My teaching is not my own, but his that sent me." "You shall know the truth and the truth shall make you freer "The spirit shall guide you into all truth."

We are immersed in mind and that mind contains all knowledge and all truth. It is seeking to give us this knowledge, for our Father delights to give good gifts to his children. The prophets and seers and great men and women, past and present, were nude great by what they received from God, not by what they were taught by men. This limitless reservoir of wisdom and power is open to you; you can draw upon it as you will, according to your needs. You can make yourself what you desire to be; you can do what you wish to do; you can have what you want. To accomplish this you must learn to become one with the Father so that you may perceive truth: so that you may have wisdom and know the right ends to seek and the right means to use to attain those ends, and so that you may secure power and ability to use the means. In closing this chapter resolve that you will now lay aside all else and concentrate upon the attainment of conscious unity with God.

Oh, when I am safe in my sylvan home, 1 tread on the pride of Greece and Rome; And when I am stretched beneath the pines, Where the evening star so holy shines, I laugh at the lore and pride of man, At the Sophist schools and the learned clan; For what are they all in their high conceit, When man in the bush with God may meet?

Chapter 5

Preparation

"Draw nigh to God and He will draw nigh to you."

If you become like God you can read his thoughts; and if you do not you will find the inspirational perception of truth impossible. You can never become a great man or woman until you have overcome anxiety, worry, and fear. It is impossible for an anxious person, a worried one, or a fearful one to perceive truth; all things are distorted and thrown out of their proper relations by such mental states, and those who are in them cannot read the thoughts of God.

If you are poor, or if you are anxious about business or financial matters, you are recommended to study carefully the first volume of this series, "The Science of Getting Rich. That will present to you a solution for your problems of this nature, no matter how large or how complicated they may seem to be.

There is not the least cause for worry about financial affairs; every person who wills to do so may rise above want, have all he needs, and become rich. The same source upon which you propose to draw for mental unfoldment and spiritual power is at your service for the supply of all your material wants. Study this truth until it is fixed in your thoughts and until anxiety is banished from your mind: enter the Certain Way, which leads to material riches.

Again, if you are anxious or worried about your health, realize it is possible for you to attain perfect health so that you way have strength sufficient for all that you wish to do and more. That Intelligence which stands ready to give you wealth and mental and spiritual power will rejoice to give you health also. Perfect health is yours for the asking, if you will only obey the simple laws of life and live aright. Conquer ill-health and cast out fear.

But it is not enough to rise above financial and physical anxiety and worry; you must rise above moral evil-doing as well. Sound your inner consciousness now for the motives which actuate you and make sure they are right. You must cast out lust, and cease to be ruled by appetite, and you must begin to govern appetite. You must eat only to satisfy hunger, never for gluttonous pleasure, and in all things you must make the flesh obey the spirit.

You must lay aside greed; have no unworthy motive in your desire to become rich and powerful. It is legitimate and right to desire riches, if you want them for the sake of the soul, but not if you desire them for the lusts of the flesh.

Cast out pride and vanity; have no thought of trying to rule over others or of outdoing them. This is a vital point; there is no temptation so insidious as the selfish desire to rule over others. Nothing so appeals to the average man or woman as to sit in the uppermost places at feasts, to be respectfully saluted in the market place, and to be called Rabbi, Master. To exercise sonic sort of control over others is the secret motive of every selfish person. The struggle for power over others is the battle of the competitive world, and you must rise above that world and its motives and aspirations and seek only for life. Cast out envy; you can have all that you want, and you need not envy any man what he has. Above all things, see to it that you do not hold malice or enmity toward anyone; to do so cuts you off from the mind whose treasures you seek to make your own. "He that loveth not his brother, loveth not God" Lay aside all narrow personal ambition and determine to seek the highest good and to be swayed by no unworthy selfishness.

Go over all the foregoing and set these moral temptations out of your heart one by one; determine to keep them out. Then resolve that you mill not only abandon all evil thought but that you will forsake all deeds, habits, and courses of action which do not commend themselves to your noblest ideals. This is supremely important; make this resolution with all the power of your soul, and you are ready for the next step toward greatness, which you will find explained in the following chapter.

Chapter 6

The Social Point of View

"Without faith it is impossible to please God," and without faith it is impossible for you to become great. The distinguishing characteristic of all really great men and women is an unwavering faith. We see this in Lincoln during the dark days of the war; we see it in Washington at Valley Forge we see it in Livingstone, the crippled missionary, threading the mazes of the dark continent, his soul aflame with the determination to let in the light upon the accursed slave trade, which his soul abhorred; we see it in Luther, and in Frances Willard, in every man and woman who has attained a place on the muster roll of the great ones of the world.

Faith – not a faith in one's self or in one's own powers but faith in principle; in the Something Great which upholds right, and which may be relied upon to give us the victory in due time. Without this faith it is not possible for anyone to rise to real greatness.

The man who has no faith in principle will always be a small man. Whether you have this faith or not depends upon your point of view. You must learn to see the world as being produced by evolution; as a something which is evolving and becoming, not as a finished work. Millions of years ago God worked with very low and crude forms of lift; low and crude, yet each perfect after its kind. Higher and more complex organisms, animal and vegetable, appeared through the successive ages; the earth passed through stage after stage in its unfoldment, each stage perfect in itself, and to be succeeded by a higher one. What I wish you to note is that the so-called "lower organisms" are as perfect after their kind as the higher ones; that the world in the Eocene period was perfect for that period; it was perfect, but God's work was not finished. This is true of the world today. Physically, socially, and industrially it is all good, and it is all perfect. It is not complete anywhere or in any part, but so far as the handiwork of God has gone it is perfect.

THIS MUST BE YOUR POINT OF VIEW: THAT THE WORLD AND ALL IT CONTAINS IS PERFECT. THOUGH NOT COMPLETED.

"All's right with the world: That is the great fact. There is nothing wrong with anything; there is nothing wrong with anybody. All the facts of life you must contemplate from this standpoint. There is nothing wrong with nature. Nature is a great advancing presence, working beneficently for the happiness of all. All things in Nature are good: she has no evil. She is not complete, for creation is still unfinished, but she is going on to give to man even more bountifully than she has given to him in the past. Nature is a partial expression of God, and God is love. She is perfect but not complete.

So of human society and government. What though there are trusts and combinations of capital and strikes and lockouts and so on. All these things are part of the forward movement; they are incidental to the evolutionary process of completing society. When it is complete there will be no more of these inharmonies; but it cannot be completed without them. J. P. Morgan is as necessary to the coming social order as the strange animals of the age of reptiles were to the life of the succeeding period, and just as these animals were perfect after their kind, so Morgan is perfect after his kind.

Behold it is all very good. See society, government, and industry as being perfect now, and as advancing rapidly toward being complete; then you will understand that there is nothing to fear, no cause for anxiety, nothing to worry about. Never complain of any of these things. They are perfect; this is the very best possible world for the stage of development man has reached.

This will sound like rank folly to many, perhaps to most people. "What!" they will say, "are not child labor and the exploitation of men and women in filthy and unsanitary factories evil things? Are not saloons evil? Do you mean to say that we shall accept all these and call them good?"

Child labor and similar things are no more evil than the way of living and the habits and practices of the cave dweller were evil. His ways were those of the savage stage of man's growth, and for that stage they were perfect. Our industrial practices are those of the savage stage of industrial development, and they are also perfect. Nothing better is possible until we cease to be mental savages in industry and business, and become men and women. This can only come about by the rise of the whole race to a higher viewpoint. And this can only come about by the rise of such individuals here and there as are ready for the higher viewpoint. The cure for all these inharmonies lies not with the masters or employers but with the workers themselves. Whenever they reach a higher viewpoint, whenever they shall desire to do so, they can establish complete brotherhood and harmony in industry: they have the numbers and the power. They are getting now what they desire. Whenever they desire more in the way of a higher, purer, more harmonious life, they will receive more. True, they want more now, but they only want more of the things that make for animal enjoyment, and so industry remains hi the savage, brutal, animal stage: when the workers begin to rise to the mental plane of living and ask for more of the things that make for the life of the mind and soul, industry will at once be raised above the plane of savagery and brutality. But it is perfect now upon its plane; behold, it is all very good.

So of saloons and dens of vice. If a majority of the people desire these things, it is right and necessary that they should have them. When a majority desire a world without such discords, they will create such a world. So long as men and women are on the plane of bestial thought, so long the social order will be in part disorder, and will show bestial manifestations. The people make society what it is, and as the people rise above the bestial thought, society will rise above the beastly in its manifestations. But a society which thinks in a bestial way must have saloons and dives; it is perfect after its kind, as the world was in the Eocene period, and very good.

All this does not prevent you from working for better things. You can work to complete an unfinished society, instead of to renovate a decaying one: and you can work with a better heart and a more hopeful spirit. It will make an immense difference with your faith and spirit whether you look upon civilization as a good thing which is becoming better or as a bad and evil thing which is decaying. One viewpoint gives you an advancing and expanding mind and the other gives you a descending and decreasing mind. One viewpoint will make you grow greater and the other will inevitably cause you to grow smaller. One will enable you to work for the eternal things: to do large works in a great way toward the completing of all that is incomplete and inharmonious: and the other will make you men' patchwork! Tint inert working almost without hope to save al few log souls from what you will grow to consider a lost and doomed world. So you see it makes a vast difference to you this matter of the social viewpoint. "All's right with the world, Nothing can possibly be wrong but my personal attitude, and I will make that right. I will sue the nets of nature and all the events, circumstances and conditions of society, politics, government, and industry from the highest viewpoint. It is all perfect, though incomplete. It is all the handiwork of God; behold, it is all very good"

Chapter 7

The Individual Point of View

Important as the matter of your point of view for the facts of social life is, it is of less moment than your viewpoint for your fellow men, for your acquaintances, friends, relatives, your immediate family, and, most of all, yourself. You must learn not to look upon the world as a lost and decaying thing but as something perfect and glorious which is going on to a most beautiful completeness: and you must learn to see men and women not as lost and accursed things, but as perfect beings advancing to become complete. There are no "bad" or "evil" people. An engine which is on the rails pulling a heavy train is perfect after its kind and it is good. The power of steam which drives it is good. Let a broken rail throw the engine into the ditch, and it does not become had or evil by being so displaced; it is a perfectly good engine, but off the track. The power of steam which drives it into the ditch and wrecks it is not evil, but a perfectly good power. So that which is misplaced or applied in an incomplete or partial way is not evil. There are no evil people; there are perfectly good people who are off the track, but they do not need condemnation or punishment; they only need to get upon the rails again.

That which is undeveloped or incomplete often appear to us as evil because of the way we have trained ourselves to think. The root of a bulb which shall produce a white lily is an unsightly thing; one might look upon it with disgust. But how foolish we should be to condemn the bulb for its appearance when we know the lily is within it. The root is perfect after its kind; it is a perfect but incomplete lily, and so we must learn to look upon every man and woman, no matter how unlovely in outward manifestation; they are perfect in their stage of being and they are becoming complete. Behold, it is all very good.

Once we come into a comprehension of this fact and arrive at this point of view, we lose all desire to find fault with people, to judge them, criticize them, or condemn them. We no longer work as those who are saving lost souls, but as those who are among the angels, working out the completion of a glorious heaven. We are born of the spirit and we see the Kingdom of God. We no longer see men as trees walking, but our vision is complete. We have nothing but good words to say. It is all good: a great and glorious humanity coming to completeness. And in our association with men this puts us into an expansive and enlarging attitude of mind; we see them as great beings and we begin to deal with them and their affairs in a great way. But if we fall to the other point of view and see a lost and degenerate race we shrink into the contracting mind; and our dealings with men and their affairs will be in a small and contracted way. Remember to hold steadily to this point of view; if you do you cannot tail to begin at once to deal with your acquaintances and neighbors and with your own family as a great personality deals with men. This same viewpoint must be the one from which you regard yourself. You must always see yourself as a great advancing soul. Learn to say: "There is THAT in me of which I am made, which knows no imperfection, weakness, or sickness. The world is incomplete, *but God in my own conscious is both perfect and complete.* Nothing can be wrong but my own personal attitude, and my own personal attitude can be wrong only when I disobey THAT which is within. I am a perfect manifestation of God so far as I have gone, and press on to be complete, I will trust and not be afraid" When you are able to say this understandingly you will have lost all fear and you will be far advanced upon the road to the development of a great and powerful personality.

Chapter 8

Consecration

Having attained to the viewpoint which puts you into the right relations with the world and with your fellow men, the next step is consecration; and consecration in its true sense simply means obedience to the soul, You have that within you which is ever impelling you toward the upward and advancing way; and that impelling something is the divine Principle of Power; you must obey it without question. No one will deny the statement that it you are to be great, the greatness must be a manifestation of something within; nor can you question that this something must be the very greatest and highest that is within. It is not the mind, or the intellect, or the reason. You cannot be great if you go no farther back for principle than to your reasoning power. Reason knows neither principle nor morality. Your reason is like a lawyer in that it will argue for either side. The intellect of a thief will plan robbery and murder as readily as the intellect of a saint will plan a great philanthropy. Intellect helps us to see the best means and manner of doing the right thing, but intellect never shows us the right thing. Intellect and reason sense the selfish man for his selfish ends as readily as they serve the unselfish man for his unselfish ends. Use intellect and reason without regard to principle, and you may become known as a very able person, but you will never become known as a person whose life shows the power of real greatness. There is too much training of the intellect anti reasoning powers and too little training in obedience to the soul. This is the only thing that can be wrong with your personal attitude – when it fails to be one of obedience to the Principle of Power.

By going back to your own center you can always find the pure idea of right for every relationship. To be great and to have power it is only necessary to conform your life to the pure idea as you find it in the GREAT WITHIN. Every compromise on this point is made at the expense of a loss of power. This you *must* remember.

There are many ideas in your mind which you have outgrown, and which, from force of habit, you still permit to dictate the actions of your life. Cease all this; abandon everything you have outgrown. There are many ignoble customs, social and other, which you still follow, although you know they tend to dwarf and belittle you and keep you acting in a small way. Rise above all this. I do not say that you should absolutely disregard conventionalities, or the commonly accepted standards of right and wrong. You cannot do this; but you can deliver your soul front most of the narrow restrictions which bind the majority of your fellow men. Do not give your time and strength to the support of obsolete institutions. religious or otherwise; do not be bound by creeds in which you do not believe. Be free. You have perhaps formed sonic" sensual habits of mind or body; abandon them. You still indulge in distrustful fears that things will go wrong, or that people will betray you, or mistreat you; get above all of them. You still act selfishly in many ways and on tinny occasions; cease to do so. Abandon all these, and in place of them put the best actions you can form a conception of in your mind. If you desire to advance, and you are not doing so, remember that it can be only because your thought is better than your practice. You must do as well as you think.

Let your thoughts be rules by principle, and then live up to your thoughts.

Let your attitude in business, in politics, in neighborhood affairs, and in your own home be the expression of the best thoughts you can think. Let your manner toward all men and women, great and small, and especially to your own family circle, always be the most kindly gracious, and courteous you can picture in your imagination. Remember your viewpoint: you are a god in the company of gods and must conduct yourself accordingly.

The steps to complete consecration are few and simple. You cannot be ruled from below if you are to be great; you must rule from above. Therefore you cannot be governed by physical impulses; you must bring your body into subjection to the mind; but your mind, without principle. may lead you into selfishness and immoral ways; you must put the mind into subjection to the soul, and your soul is limited by the boundaries of your knowledge: you must put it into subjection to that Oversold which needed no searching of the understanding but before whose eye all things are spread. That constitutes consecration. Say: "I surrender my body to be ruled by my mind; I surrender my mind to body to be ruled by my mind; I surrender my mind to be governed by my soul, and I surrender my soul to the guidance of God." Make this consecration complete and thorough, and you have taken the second great step in the way of greatness and power.

Chapter 9

Identification

Having recognized God as the advancing presence in nature, society, and your fellow men, and harmonized yourself with all these, and having consecrated yourself to that within you which impels toward the greatest and the highest, the next step is to become aware of and recognize fully the fact that the Principle of Power within you is God Himself. You must consciously identify yourself with the Highest. This is not some false or untrue position to be assumed; it is a fact to be recognized. You are already one with God; you want to become consciously aware of it.

There is one substance, the source of all things, and this substance has within itself the power that creates all things; all power is inherent in it. This substance is conscious and thinks; it works with perfect understanding and intelligence. You know that this is so, because you know that substance exists and that consciousness exists; and that it must be substance which is conscious. Man is conscious and thinks; man is substance. He must be substance, else he is nothing and does not exist at all. If man is substance and thinks, and is conscious, then he is Conscious Substance. It is not conceivable that there should be more than one Conscious Substance; so man is the original substance, the source of all life and power embodied in a physical form. Man cannot be something different from God. Intelligence is one and the same everywhere, and must be everywhere an attribute of the same substance. There cannot be one kind of intelligence in God and another kind of intelligence in man: intelligence can only be in intelligent substance, and Intelligent Substance is God. Man is of one stuff with God, and so all the talents, powers, and possibilities that are in God are in man; not in a few exceptional men but in every man. "All power is given to man, in heaven and on earth." "Is it not written, ye are gods?" The Principle of Power in man is man himself, and man himself is God. But while man is original substance, and has within him all power and possibilities, his consciousness is limited. He does not know all there is to know, and so he is liable to error and mistake. To save himself from these he must unite his mind to That outside him which does know all; he must become consciously one with God. There is a Mind surrounding him on every side, closer than breathing, nearer than hands and feet, and in this mind is the memory of all that has ever happened, from the greatest convulsions of nature in prehistoric days to the fall of a sparrow in this present time; and all that is in existence now as well. Held in this Mind is the great purpose which is behind all nature, and so it knows what is going to be. Man is surrounded by a Mind which knows all there is to know, past, present, and to come. Everything that men have said or done or written is present there. Man is of one identical stuff with this Mind; he proceeded from it; and he can so identify himself with it that he may know what it knows. "My Father is greater than I." said Jesus. "I come from him."

"I and my Father are one. He showeth the Son all things." "The Spirit shall guide you into all truth."

Your identification of yourself with the Infinite must be accomplished by conscious recognition on your part. Recognizing it as fact, that there is only God, and that all intelligence is in the one substance, you must affirm somewhat after this wise: "There is only one and that one is everywhere. I surrender myself to conscious unity with the highest. Not I, but the Father. I will to be one with the Supreme and to lead the divine life. I am one with infinite consciousness; there is but one mind, and I am that mind, I that speak unto you am he."

If you have been thorough in the work as outlined in the preceding chapters; if you have attained to the true viewpoint, and if your consecration is complete, you will not find conscious identification hard to attain; and once it is attained, the power you seek is yours, for you have made yourself one with all the power there is.

Chapter 10

Idealization

You are a thinking center in original substance, and the thoughts of original substance have creative power; whatever is formed in its thought and held as a thought-form must come into existence as a visible and so-called material form, and a thought-form held in thinking substance is a reality; it is a real thing, whether it has yet become visible to mortal eye or not. This is a fact that you should impress upon your understanding – that a thought held in thinking substance is a real thing; a form, amid has actual existence, although it is not visible to you. You internally take the form in which you think of yourself: and you surround yourself with the invisible forms of those things with which you associate in your thoughts.

If you desire a thing, picture it clearly and hold the picture steadily in mind until it becomes a definite thought-form: and if your practices are not such as to separate you from God, the thing you want will come to you in material form. It must do so in obedience to the law by which the universe was created.

Make no thought-form of yourself in connection with disease or sickness, but form a conception of health. Make a thought-form of yourself as strong and hearty and perfectly well; impress this thought form on creative intelligence, and if your practices are not in violation of the laws by which the physical body is built, your thought-form will become manifest in your flesh. This also is certain; it comes by obedience to law.

Make a thought-form of yourself as you desire to be, and set your ideal as near to perfection as your imagination is capable of forming the conception. Let me illustrate: If a young law student wishes to become great, let him picture himself (while attending to the viewpoint, consecration, and identification, as previously directed) as a great lawyer, pleading his case with matchless eloquence and power before the judge and jury; as having an unlimited command of truth, of knowledge, and of wisdom. Let him picture himself as the great lawyer in every possible situation and contingency; while he is still only the student in all circumstances, let him never forget or fail to be the great lawyer in his thought-form of himself. As the thought-form grows more definite and habitual in his mind, the creative energies, both within and without, are set at work. He begins to manifest the form from within: and all the essentials without, which go into the picture, begin to be impelled toward him. He makes himself into the image and God works with him: nothing can prevent him from becoming what he wishes to be.

In the same general way the musical student pictures himself as performing perfect harmonics, and as delighting vast audiences; the actor forms the highest conception he is capable of in regard to his art, and applies this conception to himself. The farmer and mechanic do exactly the same thing. Fix upon your idea of what you wish to make of yourself: consider well and be sure that you make the right choice; that is, the one which will be the most satisfactory to you in a general way. Do not pay too much attention to the advice or suggestions of those around you; do not believe that anyone can know, better than yourself, what is right for you. Listen to what others have to say, but always form your own conclusions. DO NOT LET OTHER PEOPLE DECIDE WHAT YOU ARE TO BE. BE WHAT YOU FEEL THAT YOU WANT TO BE.

Do not be misled by a false notion of obligation or duty. You can owe no possible obligation or duty to others which should prevent you from making the most of yourself. Be true to yourself, and you cannot then be false to any man. When you have fully decided what thing you want to be, form the highest conception of that thing that you are capable of imagining, and make that conception a thought-form. Hold that thought form as a fact, as the real truth about yourself, and believe in it.

Close your can to all adverse suggestions. Never mind if people call you a fool and a dreamer. Dream on. Remember that Bonaparte, the half-starved lieutenant, always saw himself as the general of armies and the master of France, and he became in outward realization what he held himself to be in mind. So likewise will you. Attend carefully to all that has been said in the preceding chapters, and act as directed in following ones, and will become what you want to be.

Chapter 11

Realization

If you were to stop with the close of the last chapter, however, you would never become great; you would be indeed a mere dreamer of dreams, a castle-builder. Too many do stop there; they do not understand the necessity for present action in realizing the vision and bringing the thought-form into manifestation. Two things are necessary. First, the making of the thought-form, and, second, the actual appropriation to yourself of all that goes into and around the thought-form. We have discussed the first, now we will proceed to give directions for the second. When you have made your thought-form, you are already, in your interior, what you want to be; next you must become externally what you want to be. You are already great within, but you are not yet doing the great things without. You cannot begin, on the instant, to do the great things; you cannot be before the world the great actor, or lawyer, or musician, or personality you know yourself to be; no one will entrust great things to you as yet for you have not nude yourself known. But you can always begin to do small things in a great way.

Here lies the whole secret. You can begin to be great today in your own home, in your store or office, on the street, everywhere; you can begin to make yourself known as great, and you can do this by doing everything you do in a great way. You must put the whole power of your great soul into every act, however small and common place, and so reveal to your family your friends, and neighbors what you really are. Do not brag or boast of yourself: do not go about telling people what a great personage you are; simply live in a great way. No one will believe you if you tell him you are a great man, but no one can doubt your greatness if you show it in your actions. In your domestic circle be so just, so generous, so courteous, and kindly that your family, your wife, husband, children, brothers, and sisters shall know that you are a great and noble soul. In all your relations with men be great, just, generous, courteous, and kindly. The great are never otherwise. This for your attitude.

Next, and most important, you must have absolute faith in your own perceptions of truth. Never act in haste or hurry; be deliberate in everything; wait until you feel that you know thc truc way. And when you do feel that you know the true way, be guided by your own faith though all the world skill disagree with you. If you do not believe what God tells you in little things, you will never draw upon his wisdom and knowledge in larger things. When you feel deeply that a certain act is the right act, do it and have perfect faith that the consequences will be good. When you are deeply impressed that a certain thing is true, no matter what the appearances to the contrary may be, accept that thing as true and act accordingly. The one way to develop a perception of truth in large things is to trust absolutely to your present perception of truth in small things. Remember that you are seeking to develop this very power or faculty – the perception of truth; you are learning to read the thoughts of God. Nothing is great and nothing is small in the sight of Omnipotence; he holds the sun in its place, but he also notes a sparrow's fall, and numbers the hairs of your head. God is as much interested in the little matters of everyday life as he is in the affairs of nations. You can perceive truth about family and neighborhood affairs as well as about matters of statecraft. And the way to begin is to have perfect faith in the truth in these small matters, as it is revealed to you from day to day. When you feel deeply impelled to take a course which seems contrary to all reason and worldly judgment, take that course. Listen to the suggestions and advice of others, but always do what you feel deeply in the within to be the true thing to do. Rely with absolute faith, at all times, on your own perception of truth; but be sure that you listen to God – that you do not act in haste, fear, or anxiety.

Rely upon your perception of truth in all the facts and circumstances of life. If you deeply feel that a certain man will be in a certain place on a certain day, go there with perfect faith to meet him; he will be there, no matter how unlikely it may seem. If you feel sure that certain people are making certain combinations, or doing certain things, act in the faith that they are doing those things. If you feel sure of the truth of any circumstance or happening, near or distant, past, present, or to come, trust in your perception. You may make occasional mistakes at first because of your imperfect understanding of the within; but you will soon be guided almost invariably right. Soon your family and friends will begin to defer, more and more, to your judgment and to be guided by you. Soon your neighbors and townsmen will be coming to you for counsel and advice; soon you will be recognised as one who is great in small things, and I will be called upon more and more to take charge of larger things. All that is necessary is to be guided absolutely, in all things, by your inner light, your perception of truth. Obey your soul, have perfect faith in yourself. Never think of yourself with doubt or distrust, or as one who makes mistakes. "If I judge, my judgment is just, for I seek not honor from men, but from the Father only."

Chapter 12

Hurry and Habit

No doubt you have many problems, domestic, social, physical, and financial, which seem to you to be pressing for instant solution. You have debts which must be paid, or other obligations which must be met; you are unhappily or inharmoniously placed, and feel that something must be done at once. Do not get into a hurry and act from superficial impulses. You can trust God for the solution of all your personal riddles. There is no hurry. There is only God, and all is well with the world.

There is an invincible power in you, and the same power is in the things you want. It is bringing them to you and bringing you to them. This is a thought that you must grasp, and hold continuously – that the same intelligence which is in you is in the think you desire. They are impelled toward you as strongly and decidedly as your desire impels you toward them.

The tendency, therefore, of a steadily held thought must be to bring the things you desire to you and to group them around you. So long as you hold your thought and your faith right all must go well. *Nothing can be wrong but your own personal attitude, and that will not be wrong if you trust and are not afraid.* Hurry is a manifestation of fear; he who fears not has plenty of time. If you act with perfect faith in your own perceptions of truth, you will never be too late or too early; and nothing will go wrong. If things appear to be going wrong, do not get disturbed in mind; it is only in appearance. Nothing can go wrong in this world but yourself: and you can go wrong only by getting into the wrong mental attitude. Whenever you find yourself getting excited, worried, or into the mental attitude of hurry sit down and think it over; play a game of some kind, or take a vacation. Go on a trip, and all will be right when you return. So surely as you find yourself in the mental attitude of haste, just so surely may you know that you are out of the mental attitude of greatness. Hurry and fear will instantly cut your connection with the universal mind; you will get no power, no wisdom, and no information until you are calm. And to fill into the attitude of hurry will check the action of the Principle of Power within you. Fear turns strength to weakness.

Remember that poise and power are inseparably associated. The calm and balanced mind is the strong and great mind; the hurried and agitated mind is the weak one. Whenever you fall into the mental state of hurry you may know that you have lost the right viewpoint; you are beginning to look upon the world, or some part of it, as going wrong. At such times read

Chapter Six of this book; consider the fact that this world is perfect, now, with all that it contains. Nothing is going wrong; nothing can be wrong; be poised, be calm, be cheerful: have faith in God.

Next, as to habit. It is probable that your greatest difficulty will be to overcome your old habitual ways of thought, and to form new habits. The world is ruled by habit. Kings, tyrants, masters, and plutocrats hold their positions solely because the people have come to habitually accept them. Things are as they are only because people have formed the habit of accepting them as they are. When the people change their habitual thought about governmental, social, and industrial institutions, they will change the institutions. Habit rules us all.

You have formed, perhaps, the habit of thinking of yourself as a common person, as one of a limited ability or as being more or less of a failure. Whatever you habitually think yourself to be, that you are. You must form, now, a greater and better habit; you must form a conception of yourself as a being of limitless power, and habitually think that you are that being. It is the habitual, not the periodical thought that decides your destiny. It will avail you nothing to sit apart for a few moments several times a day to affirm that you are great, if during all the balance of the day, while you are about your regular vocation, you think of yourself as not great. No amount of praying or affirmation will make you great if you still habitually regard yourself as being small.

The use of prayer and affirmation is to change your habit of thought. Any act, mental or physical, often repeated, becomes a habit. The purpose of mental exercises is to repeat certain thoughts over and over until the thinking of those thoughts becomes constant and habitual. The thoughts we continually repeat become convictions. What you must do is to repeat the new thought of yourself until it is the only way in which you think of yourself. Habitual thought, and not environment or circumstance has made you what you are. Every person has some central idea or thought-form of himself; and by this idea he classifies and arranges all his facts and external relationships. You are classifying your facts either according to the idea that you are a great and strong personality, or according to the idea that you are limited, common, or weak. If the latter is the use you must change your central idea. Get a new mental picture of yourself. Do not try to become great by repeating mere strings of words or superficial formulae: but repeat over and over the THOUGHT of your own power and ability until you classify external facts, and decide your place everywhere by this idea. In another chapter will be found an illustrative mental exercise and further directions on this point.

Chapter 13

Thought

Greatness is attained only by the thinking of great thoughts. No man can become great in outward personality until he is great internally; and no man can be great internally until he THINKS. No amount of education, reading, or study can make you great without thought; but thought can make you great with very little study. There are altogether too many people who are trying to make something of themselves by reading books without thinking; all such will fail. You are not mentally developed by what you read, but by what you think about what you read.

Thinking is the hardest and most exhausting of all labor; and hence many people shrink from it. God has so formed us that we are continuously impelled to thought; we must either think or engage in some activity to escape thought. The headlong, continuous chase for pleasure in which most people spend all their leisure time is only an effort to escape thought. If they are alone, or if they have nothing amusing to take their attention, as a novel to read or a show to see, they must think; and to escape from thinking they resort to novels, shows, and all the endless devices of the purveyors of amusement. Most people spend the greater part of their leisure time running away from thought, hence they are where they are. We never move forward until we begin to think.

Read less and think more. Read about great things and think about great questions and issues. We have at the present time few really great figures in the political life of our country; our politicians are a petty lot. There is no Lincoln, no Webster, no Clay, Calhoun, or Jackson. Why? Because our present statesmen deal only with sordid and petty issues – questions of dollars and cents, of expediency and party success, of material prosperity without regard to ethical right. Thinking along these lines does not call forth great souls. The statesmen of Lincoln's time and previous times dealt with questions of eternal truth: of human rights and justice. Men thought upon great themes; they thought great thoughts, and they became great men.

Thinking, not mere knowledge or information, makes personality. Thinking is growth: you cannot think without growing. Every thought engenders another thought. Write one idea and others will follow until you have written a page. You cannot fathom your own mind: it has neither bottom or boundaries. Your first thoughts may be crude: but as you go on thinking you will use more and more of yourself: you will quicken new brain cells into activity and you will develop new faculties.

Heredity, environment, circumstances – all things must give way before you if you practice sustained and continuous thought. But, on the other hand, if you neglect to think for yourself and only use other people's thought, you will never know what you are capable oil and you will end by being in capable of anything.

There can be no real greatness without original thought. All that a man does outwardly is the expression and completion of his inward thinking. No action is possible without thought, and no great action is possible until a great thought has preceded it. Action is the second form of thought, and personality is the materialization of thought. Environment is the result of thought; things group themselves or arrange themselves around you according to your thought. There is, as Emerson says, some central idea or conception of yourself by which all the facts of your life are arranged and classified. Change this central idea and you change the arrangement or classification of all the facts and circumstances of your life. You are what you are because you think as you do; you are where you are because you think as you do.

You see then the immense importance of thinking about the great essentials set forth in the preceding chapters. You must not accept them in any superficial way; you must think about them until they are a part of your central idea. Go back to the matter of the point of view and consider, in all its bearings, the tremendous thought that you live in a perfect world among perfect people, and that nothing can possibly be wrong with you but your own personal attitude. Think about all this until you fully realize all that it means to you. Consider that this is God's world and that it is the best of all possible worlds; that He has brought it thus far toward completion by the processes of organic, social, and industrial evolution, and that it is going on to greater completeness and harmony. Consider that there is one great, perfect, intelligent Principle of Life and Power, causing all the changing phenomena of the cosmos. Think about all this until you see that it is true, and until you comprehend how you should live and act as a citizen of such a perfect whole.

Next, think of the wonderful truth that this great Intelligence is in you; it is your own intelligence. It is an Inner Light impelling you toward the right thing and the best thing, the greatest act, and the highest happiness. It is a Principle of Power in you, giving you all the ability and genius there is. It will infallibly guide you to the best if you will submit to it and walk in the light. Consider what is meant by your consecration of yourself when you say: "I will obey my soul."This is a sentence of tremendous meaning; it must revolutionize the attitude and behaviour of the average person.

Then think of your identification with this Great Supreme; that all its knowledge is yours, and all its wisdom is yours, for the asking. You are a god if you think like a god. If you think like a god you cannot fail to act like a god. Divine thoughts will surely externalize themselves in a divine life. Thoughts of power will end in a life of power. Great thoughts will manifest in a great personality. Think well of all this, and then you are ready to act.

Chapter 14

Action at Home

Do not merely think that you are going to become great; think *that you are great now*. Do not think that you will begin to act in a great way at some future time; begin now. Do not think that you will act in a great way when you reach a different environment; act in a great way where you are now. Do not think that you will begin to act in a great way when you begin to deal with great things; begin to deal in a great way with small things. Do not think that you will begin to be great when you get among more intelligent people, or among people who understand you better; begin now to deal in a great may with the people around you.

If you are not in an environment where there is scope for your best powers and talents you can move in due time: but meanwhile you can be great where you are. Lincoln was as great when he was a backwoods lawyer as when he was President:

as a backwoods lawyer he did common things in a great way, and that made him President. Had he waited until he reached Washington to begin to be great, he would have remained unknown. You are not made great by the location in which you happen to be, nor by the things with which you may surround yourself. You are not made great by what you receive from others, and you can never manifest greatness so long as you depend on others. You will manifest greatness only when you begin to stand alone. Dismiss all thought of reliance on externals, whether things, books, or people. As Emerson said, "Shakespeare will never be made by the study of Shakespeare." Shakespeare will be made by the thinking of Shakespearean thoughts.

Never mind how the people around you, including those of your own household, may treat you. That has nothing at all to do with your being great; that is, it cannot hinder you from being great. People may neglect you and be unthankful and unkind in their attitude toward you; does that prevent you from being great in your manner and attitude toward them?

"Your Father." said Jesus. "is kind to the unthankful and the evil." Would God be great if he should go away and sulk because people were unthankful and did not appreciate him? Treat the unthankful and the evil in a great and perfectly kind way, just as God does.

Do not talk about your greatness: you are really, in essential nature, no greater than those around you. You may have entered upon a way of living and thinking which they have not yet found, but they are perfect on their own plane of thought and action. You are entitled to no special honor or consideration for your greatness. You are a god, but you are among gods. You will fall into the boastful attitude if you see other people's shortcomings and failures and compare them with your own virtues and successes; and if you fall into the boastful attitude of mind, you will cease to be great, and become small. Think of yourself as a perfect being among perfect beings, and meet every person as an equal, not as either a superior or an inferior. Give yourself no airs; great people never do. Ask no honors and seek for no recognition; honors and recognition will come fast enough if you are en titled to them.

Begin at home. It is a great person who can always be poised, assured, calm, and perfectly kind and considerate at home. If your manner and attitude in your own family are always the best you can think, you will soon become the one on whom all the others will rely. You will be a tower of strength and a support in time of trouble. You will be loved and appreciated. At the same time do not make the mistake of throwing yourself away in the service of others. The great person respects himself; he serves and helps, but he is never slavishly servile. You cannot help your family by being a slave to them, or by doing for them those things which by right they should do for themselves. You do a person an injury when you wait on him too much. The selfish and exacting are a great deal better off if their exactions are denied. The ideal world is not one where there are a lot of people being waited on by other people; it is a world where everybody waits on himself. Meet all demands, selfish and otherwise, with perfect kindness and consideration; but do not allow yourself to be made a slave to the whims, caprices, exactions, or slavish desires of any member of your family. To do so is not great, and it works an injury to the other party.

Do not become uneasy over the failures or mistakes of any member of your family, and feel that you must interfere. Do not be disturbed if others seem to be going wrong, and feel that you must step in and set them right. Remember that every person is perfect on his own plane; you cannot improve on the work of God. Do not meddle with the personal habits and practices of others, though they are your nearest and dearest; these things are none of your business. Nothing can be wrong but your own personal attitude; make that right and you will know that all else is right. You are a truly great soul when you can live with those who do things which you do not do, and yet refrain from either criticism or interference. Do the things which are right for you to do, and believe that every member of your family is doing the things which are right for him. Nothing is wrong with anybody or anything; behold, it is all very good. Do not be enslaved by anyone else, but be just as careful that you do not enslave anyone else to your own notions of what is right.

Think, and think deeply and continuously; be perfect in your kindness and consideration; let your attitude be that of a god among gods, and not of a god among inferior beings. This is the way to be great in your own home.

Chapter 15

Action Abroad

The rules which apply to your action at home must apply to your action everywhere. Never forget for an instant that this is a perfect world, and that you are a god among gods. You are as great as the greatest, but all are your equals.

Rely absolutely on your perception of truth. Trust to the inner light rather than to reason, but be sure that your perception comes from the inner light; act in poise and calmness; be still and attend on God. Your identification of yourself with the All-Mind will give you all the knowledge you need for guidance in any contingency which may arise in your own life or in the lives of others. It is only necessary that you should be supremely calm, and rely upon the eternal wisdom winch is within you. It you act in poise and faith, your judgment will always be right, and you will always know exactly what to do. Do not hurry or sorry; remember Lincoln in the dark days of the war. James Freeman Clarke relates that after the battle of Fredericksburg, Lincoln alone furnished a supply of faith and hope for the nation. Hundreds of leading men, from all parts of the country, went sadly into his room and came out cheerful and hopeful. They had stood face to face with the Highest, and had seen God in this lank, ungainly, patient man, although they knew it not.

Have perfect faith in yourself and in your own ability to cope with any combination of circumstances that may arise. Do not be disturbed if you are alone; if you need friends they will be brought to you at the right time. Do not be disturbed if you feel that you are ignorant; the information that you need will be furnished you when it is time for you to have it. That which is in you impelling you forward is in the things and people you need, impelling them toward you. It there is a particular man you need to know, he will be introduced to you: if there is a particular book you need to read it will be placed in your hands at the right time. All the knowledge you need will come to you from both external and internal sources. Your information and your talents will always be equal to the requirements of the occasion. Remember that Jesus told his disciples not to worry as to what they should say when brought before the judges; he knew that the power in them would be sufficient for the needs of the hour. As soon as you awaken and begin to use your faculties in a great way you will apply power to the development of your brain; new cells will be created and dormant cells quickened into activity, and your brain will be qualified as a perfect instrument for your mind.

Do not try to do great things until you are ready to go about them in a great way. If you undertake to deal with great matters in a small way – that is, from a low viewpoint or with incomplete consecration and wavering faith and courage – you will fail. Do not be in a hurry to get to the great things. Doing great things will not make you great, but becoming great will certainly lead you to the doing of great things. Begin to be great where you are and in the things you do every day. Do not be in haste to be found out or recognized as a great personality. Do not be disappointed if men do not nominate you for office within a month after you begin to practice what you read in this book. Great people never seek for recognition or applause: they are not great because they want to be paid for being so. Greatness is reward enough for itself; the joy of bring something and of knowing that you are advancing is the greatest of all joys possible to man.

If you begin in your own family, as described in the preceding chapter, and then assume the same menu! Attitude with your neighbors, friends, and those you meet in business, you will soon find that people are beginning to depend on you. Your advice will he sought, and a constantly increasing number of people will look to you for strength and inspiration, and rely upon your judgment. Here, as in the home, you must avoid meddling with other people's affairs. Help all who come to you, but do not go about officiously endeavoring to set other people right. Mind your own business. It is no part of your mission in life to correct people's morals, habits, or practices. Lead a great life, doing all things with a great spirit and in a great way; give to him that asketh of thee as freely as ye have received, but do not force your help or your opinions upon any man. If your neighbor wishes to smoke or drink, it is his business; it is none of yours until he consults you about it. If you lead a great life and do no preaching, you will save a thousand times as many souls as one who leads a small life and preaches continuously.

If you hold the right viewpoint of the world, others will find it out and be impressed by it through your daily conversation and practice. Do not try to convert others to your point of view, except by holding it and living accordingly. If your consecration is perfect you do not need to tell anyone; it will speedily become apparent to all that you are guided by a higher principle than the average man or woman. If your identification with God is complete, you do not need to explain the fact to others; it will become self-evident. To become known as a great personality, you have nothing to do but to live. Do not imagine that you must go charging about the world like Don Quixote, tilting at windmills, and overturning things in general, in order to demonstrate that you are somebody. Do not go hunting for big things to do. Live a great life where you are, and in the daily work you have to do, and greater works will surely find you out. Big things will come to you, asking to be done.

Be so impressed with the value of a man that you treat even a beggar or the tramp with the most distinguished consideration. All is God. Every man and woman is perfect. Let your manner be that of a god addressing other gods. Do not save all your consideration for the poor; the millionaire is as good as the tramp. This is perfectly good world, and there is not a person or thing in it but is exactly right; be sure that you keep this in mind in dealing with things and men.

Form your mental vision of yourself with care. Make the thought-form of yourself as you wish to be, and hold this with the faith that it is being realized, and with the purpose to realize it completely, Do every common act as a god should do it; speak every word as a god should speak it; meet men and women of both low and high estate as a god meets other divine beings. Begin thus and continue thus, and your unfoldment in ability and power will be great and rapid.

Chapter 16

Some Further Explanations

We go back here to the matter of the point of view, for, besides being vitally important, it is the one which is likely to give the student the most trouble. We have been trained. partly by mistaken religious teachers, to look upon the world as being like a wrecked ship, storm-driven upon a rocky coast; inter destruction is inevitable at the end, and the most that can be done is to rescue, perhaps, a few of the crew. This view teaches us to consider the world as essentially bad and growing worse; and to believe that existing discords and inharmonies must continue and intensify until the end. It robs us of hope for society, government, and humanity, and gives us a decreasing outlook and contracting mind.

This is all wrong. The world is not wrecked. It is like a magnificent steamer with the engines in place and the machinery in perfect order. The bunkers are full of coal, and the ship is amply provisioned for the cruise; there is no lack of any good thing. Every provision Omniscience could devise has been made for the safety, comfort, and happiness of the crew; the steamer is out on the high seas tacking hither and thither because no one has yet learned the right course to steer. We are learning to steer, and in due time will come grandly into the harbor of perfect harmony.

The world is good, and growing better. Existing discords and inharmonies are but the railings of the ship incidental to our own imperfect steering; they will all be removed in due time. This view gives us an increasing outlook and an expanding mind: it enables us to think largely of society and of ourselves, and to do thing in a great way.

Furthermore, we see that nothing can be wrong with such a world or with any part of it, including our own affairs. If it is all moving on toward completion, then it is not going wrong; and as our own personal affairs are a part of the whole, they are not going wrong. You and all that you are concerned with are moving on toward completeness. Nothing can check this forward movement but yourself: and you can only check it by assuming a mental attitude which is at cross purposes with the mind of God. You have nothing to keep right but yourself if you keep yourself right, nothing can possibly go wrong with you, and you can have nothing to fear. No business or other disaster can come upon you if your personal attitude is right, for you are a part of that which is increasing and advancing, and you must increase and advance with it.

Moreover your thought-form will be mostly shaped according to your viewpoint of the cosmos. If you see the world as a lost and ruined thing you will see yourself as a part of it, and as partaking of its sins and weaknesses. If your outlook for the world as a whole is hopeless, your outlook for yourself cannot be hopeful. If you see the world as declining toward its end, you cannot see yourself as advancing. Unless you think well of all the works of God you cannot really think well of yourself, and unless you think well of yourself you can never become great.

I repeat that your place in life, including your material environment, is determined by the thought-form you habitually hold of yourself. When you make a thought-form of yourself you can hardly fail to thrill in your mind a corresponding environment. If you think of yourself as an incapable, inefficient person, you will think of yourself with poor or cheap surroundings. Unless you think well of yourself you will be sure to picture yourself in a more or less poverty stricken environment. These thoughts, habitually held, become invisible forms in the surrounding mind-stuff, and are with you continually. In due time, by the regular action of the eternal creative energy, the invisible thought-forms are produced in material stuff, and you are surrounded by your own thoughts made into material things.

See nature as a great living and advancing presence, and see human society in exactly the same way. It is all one, coming from one source, and it is all good. You yourself are made of the same stuff as God. All the constituents of God are parts of yourself; every power that God has is a constituent of man. You can move forward as you see God doing. You have within yourself the source of every power.

Chapter 17

More about Thought

I give place here to some further consideration of thought. You will never become great until your own thoughts make you great, and therefore it is of the first importance that you should THINK. You will never do great things in the external world until you think great things in the intend world; and you will never think great things until you think about *truth*; about the verities. To think great things you must be absolutely sincere; and to be sincere you must know that your intentions are right. Insincere or false thinking is never great, however logical and brilliant it may be.

The first and most important step is to seek the truth about human relations; to know what you ought to be to other men, and what they ought to be to you. This brings you back to the search for a right viewpoint. You should study organic and social evolution. Read Darwin and Walter Thomas Mills, and when you read. THINK; think the whole matter over until you see the world of things and men in the right way. THINK about what God is doing until you can SEE what he is doing.

Your next step is to think yourself into the right personal attitude. Your viewpoint tells you what the right attitude is, and obedience to the soul puts you into it. It is only by making a complete consecration of yourself to the highest that is within you that you can attain to sincere thinking. So long as you know you are selfish in your aims, or dishonest or crooked in any way in your intentions or practices, your thinking will be false and your thoughts will have no power. THINK about the way you are doing things; about all your intentions, purposes, and practices, until you know that they are right.

The fact of his own complete unity with God is one that no person can grasp without deep and sustained thinking. Anyone can accept the proposition in superficial way, but to feel and realize a vital comprehension of it is another matter. It is easy to think of going outside of yourself to meet God, but it is not so easy to think of going inside yourself to meet God. But God is there, and in the holy of holies of your own soul you any meet him face to face. It is a tremendous thing, this fact that all you need is already within you; that you do not have to consider how to get the power to do what you want to do or to make yourself what you want to be. You have only to consider how to use the power you have in the right way. And there is nothing to do but to begin. Use your perception of truth; you can see some truth today: live fully up to that and you will see more truth tomorrow.

To rid yourself of the old false ideas you will have to think a great deal about the value of men – the greatness and worth of a human soul. You must cease from looking at mistakes and look at successes; cease from seeing faults and see virtues. You can no longer look upon men and women as lost and ruined beings who are descending into hell; you must come to regard them as shining souls who are ascending toward heaven. It will require some exercise of will power to do this, but this is the legitimate use of the will – to decide what you will think about and how you will think.

The function of the will is to direct thought. Think about the good side of men; the lovely, attractive part, and exert your will in refining to think of anything else in connection with them.

I know of no one who has attained to so much on this one point as Eugene V. Debs, twice the Socialist candidate for president of the United States. Mr. Debs reverences humanity. No appeal for help is ever made to him in vain. No one receives from him an unkind or censorious word. You cannot come into his presence without being nude sensible of his deep and kindly personal interest in you. No one, whether millionaire, grimy workingman, or toil worn woman, receives the radiant warmth of a brotherly affection that is sincere and true. No ragged child speaks to him on the street without receiving instant and tender recognition. Debs loves men. This has made him the leading figure in a great movement, the beloved hero of a million hearts, and will give him a deathless name. It is a great thing to love men so and it is only achieved by thought. Nothing can make you great but thought.

We may divide thinkers into those who think for themselves and those who think through others. The latter are the rule and the former the exception. The first are original thinkers in a double sense, and egotists in the noblest meaning of the word.

—Schopenhauer

The key to every man is his thought. Sturdy and defiant though he look he has a helm which he obeys, which is the idea after which all his facts are classified. He can only be reformed by showing him a new idea which commands his own.

—Emerson

All truly wise thoughts have been thought already thousands of times; but to make them really ours we must think them over again honestly till they take root in our personal expression.

—Goethe

All that a man is outwardly is but the expression and completion of his inward thought. To work effectively he must think clearly. To act nobly he must think nobly.

—Charming

Great men are they who see that spirituality is stronger than any material force; that thoughts rule the world.

—Emerson

Some people study all their lives, and at their death they have learned everything except to think.

—Domergue

It is the habitual thought that frames itself into our life. It affects us even more than our intimate social relations do. Our confidential friends have not so much to do in shaping our lives as the thoughts have which we harbor.

—J. W. Teal

When God lets loose a great thinker on this planet, then all things are at risk. There is not a piece of science but its flank may be turned tomorrow; nor any literary reputation or the so-called eternal names of fame that may not be refused and condemned.

—Emerson

Think! *Think!!* THINK!!!

Chapter 18

Jesus' Idea of Greatness

In the twenty-third chapter of Matthew Jesus makes a very plain distinction between true and false greatness; and also points out the one great danger to all who wish to become great – the most insidious of temptations which all must avoid and fight unceasingly who desire to really climb in the world. Speaking to the multitude and to his disciples he bids them beware of adopting the principle of the Pharisees. He points out that while the Pharisees are just and righteous men, honorable judges, true lawgivers and upright in their dealings with men, they "love the uppermost seats at feasts and greetings in the market place, and to be called Master, Master": and in comparison with this principle, he says: "He that will be great among you let him serve."

The average person's idea of a great man, rather than of one who serves, is of one who succeeds in getting himself served. He gets himself in a position to command men: to exercise power over them, making them obey his will. The exercise of dominion over other people, to most persons, is a great thing. Nothing seems to be sweeter to the selfish soul than this. You will always find every selfish and undeveloped person trying to domineer over others, to exercise control over other men. Savage men were no sooner placed upon the earth than they began to enslave one another. For ages the struggle in war, diplomacy, politics, and government has been aimed at the securing of control over oilier men. King and princes have drenched the soil of the earth in blood and tears in the calm to extend their dominions and their power – to rule more people.

The struggle of the business world today is the same as that on the battlefields of Europe a century ago so far as the ruling principle is concerned. Robert G. Ingersoll could not understand why men like Rockefeller and Carnegie seek for more money and make themselves slaves to the business struggle when they already have more than they can possibly use. He thought it a kind of madness and illustrated it as follows: "Suppose a man had fifty thousand pairs of pants, seventy-five thousand vests, one hundred thousand coats, and one hundred and fifty thousand neckties, what would you think of him if he arose in the morning before light and worked until after it was dark every day, rain or shine, in all kinds of weather, merely to get another necktie?"

But it is not a good simile. The possession of neckties gives a man no power over other men, while the possession of dollars does. Rockefeller, Carnegie, and their kind are not after dollars but power. It is the principle of the Pharisee; it is the struggle for the high place. It develops able men, cunning men, resourceful men, but not great men.

I want you to contrast these two ideas of greatness sharply in your minds. "He that will be great among you let him serve." Let me stand before the average American audience and ask the name of the greatest American and the majority will think of Abraham Lincoln; and is this not because in Lincoln above all the other met, who have served us in public life we recognize the spirit of service? Not servility, but service. Lincoln was a great man because he knew how to be a great servant. Napoleon, able, cold, selfish, seeking the high places, was a brilliant man. Lincoln was great, Napoleon was not.

The very moment you begin to advance and are recognized as one who is doing things in a great way you will find yourself in danger. The temptation to patronize, advise, or take upon yourself the direction of other people's affairs is sometimes almost irresistible. Avoid, however, the opposite danger of falling into servility, or of completely throwing yourself away in the service of others. To do this has been the ideal of a great many people. The completely self-sacrificing life has been thought to be the Christ-like life, because, as I think, of a complete misconception of the character and teachings of Jesus. I have explained this misconception in a little book which I hope you may all sometime read.[1] Thousands of people imitating Jesus, as they suppose, have belittled themselves and given up all else to go about doing good: practicing

1. A New Christ

an altruism that is really as morbid and as far from great as the rankest selfishness. The finer instincts which respond to the cry of trouble or distress are not by any means all of you; they are riot necessarily the best part of you. There are other things you must do besides helping the unfortunate, although it is true that a large part of the life and activities of every great person must be given to helping other people. As you begin to advance they will come to you. Do not turn them away. But do not make the fatal error of supposing that the lift of complete self-abnegation is the way of greatness.

To make another point here, let me refer to the fact that Swedenborg's classification of fundamental motives is exactly the same as that of Jesus. He divides all men into two groups: those who live in pure love, and those who live in what he calls the love of ruling for the love of self. It will be seen that this is exactly the same as the lust for place and power of the Pharisees. Swedenborg saw this selfish love of power as the cause of all sin. It was the only evil desire of the human heart, from which all other evil desires sprang. Over against this he places pure love. He does not say love of God or love of man, but merely love. Nearly all religionists make more of love and service to God than they do of love and service to man. But it is a fact that love to God is not sufficient to save a man from the lust for power, for some of the most ardent lovers of the Deity have been the worst of tyrants. Lovers of God are often tyrants, and lovers of men are often meddlesome and officious.

Chapter 19

A View of Evolution

But how shall we avoid throwing ourselves into altruistic work if we are surrounded by poverty ignorance, suffering, and every appearance of misery as very many people are? Those who live where the withered hand of want is thrust upon them from every side appealingly for aid must find it hard to refrain from continuous giving. Again, there are social and other irregularities, injustices done to the weak, which fire generous souls with an almost irresistible desire to set things right. We want to start a crusade; we feel that the wrongs will never be righted until we give ourselves wholly to the task. In all this we must fall back upon the point of view. We must remember that this is not a bad world but a good world in the process of becoming.

Beyond all doubt there was a time when there was no life upon this earth. The testimony of geology to the fact that the globe was once a ball of burning gas and molten rock, clothed about with boiling vapors, is indisputable. And we do not know how life could have existed under such conditions; that seems impossible. Geology tells us that later on a crust formed, the globe cooled and hardened, the vapors condensed and became mist or fell in rain. The cooled surface crumbled into soil; moisture accumulated, ponds and seas were gathered together, and at last somewhere in the water or on the land appeared something that was alive.

It is reasonable to suppose that this first life was in single-celled organisms, but behind these cells was the insistent urge of Spirit, the Great One Life seeking expression. And soon organisms having too much life to express themselves with one cell had two cells and then many, and still more life was poured into them.

Multiple-celled organisms were formed; plains, trees, vertebrates, and mammals, many of them with strange shapes, but all were perfect after their kind as everything is that God makes. No doubt there were crude and almost monstrous forms of both animal and plant life; but everything filled its purpose in its day and it was all very good.

Then another day came, the great day of the evolutionary process, a day when the morning stars sang together and the sons of God shouted for joy to behold the beginning of the end, for man, the object aimed at from the beginning, had appeared upon the scene. An ape-like being, little different from the beasts around him in appearance but infinitely different in his capacity for growth and thought. Art and beauty, architecture and song, poetry and music, all these were unrealized possibilities in that ape-man's soul. And for his time and kind he was very good.

"It is God that works in you to will and to do of his good pleasure," says St. Paul. From the day the first man appeared God began to work IN men, putting more and more of himself into each succeeding generation, urging them on to larger achievements and to better conditions, social, governmental, and domestic. Those who looking back into ancient history see the awful conditions which existed, the barbarities, idolatries, and sufferings, and reading about God in connection with their things are disposed to feel that he was cruel and unjust to man, should pause to think. From the ape-man to the coming Christ man the race has had to rise. And it could only be accomplished by the successive unfoldments of the various powers and possibilities latent in the human brain. Naturally the cruder and snore animal-like part of man came to its full development first; for ages men were brutal; their governments were brutal, their religions were brutal, their domestic institutions were brutal, and what appears to be an immense amount of suffering resulted from this brutality. But God never delighted in suffering, and in every age he has given men a message, telling them how to avoid it. And all the while the urge of life, insistent, powerful, compelling, made the race keep moving forward; a little less brutality in each age and a little more spirituality in each age. And God kept on working in man. In every age there have been some individuals who were in advance of the mass and who heard and understood God better than their fellows. Upon these the inspiring hand of Spirit was laid and they were compelled to become interpreters.

These were the prophets and seen, sometimes the priests and kings, and oftener still they were martyrs driven to the stake, the block, or the cross. It is to these who have heard God, spoken his word, and demonstrated his truth in their lives that all progress is really due.

Again, considering for a moment the presence of what is called evil in the world, we see that that which appears to us to be evil is only undeveloped; and that the undeveloped is perfectly good in its own stage and place. Because all things are necessary to man's complete unfoldment, all things in human life are the work of God. The graft rings in our cities, the red-light districts and their unfortunate inmates, these he consciously and voluntarily produced. Their part in the plan of unfoldment must be played. And when their pan has been played he will sweep them off the stage as he did the strange and poisonous monsters which filled the swamps of the past ages.

In concluding this vision of evolution we might ask why it was all done, what is it for? This question should be easy for the thoughtful mind to answer. God desired to express himself, to live in form, and not only that, but to live in a form through which he could express himself on the highest moral and spiritual plane. God wanted to evolve a form in which he could live as a god and manifest himself as a god. This was the aim of the evolutionary force. The ages of warfare, bloodshed, suffering, injustice, and cruelty were tempered in many ways with love and justice as time advanced. And this was developing the brain of man to a point where it should he capable of giving full expression to the love and justice of God. The end is not yet; God aims not at the perfection of a few choice specimens for exhibition, like the large berries at the top of the box, but at the glorification of the race. The time will come when the Kingdom of God shall be established on earth; the time foreseen by the dreamer of the Isle of Patmos, when there shall be no more crying, neither shall there be any more pain, for the former things are all passed away and there shall be no night there.

Chapter 20

Serving God

I have brought you thus far through the two preceding chapters with a view to finally settling the question of duty. This is one that puzzles and perplexes very many people who are earnest and sincere, and gives them a great deal of difficulty in its solution.

When they start out to make something of themselves and to practice the science of being great, they find themselves necessarily compelled to rearrange many of their relationships.

There are friends who perhaps must be alienated, there are relatives who misunderstand and who feel that they are in some way being slighted; the really great man is often considered selfish by a large circle of people who are connected with him and who feel that he might bestow upon them more benefits than be does. The question at the outset is: Is it my duty to make the most of myself regardless of everything else?

Or shall I wait until I can do so without any friction or without causing loss to anyone? This is the question of duty to self vs. duty to others.

One's duty to the world has been thoroughly discussed in the preceding pages and I give some consideration now to the idea of duty to God. An immense number of people have a great deal of uncertainty, not to say anxiety; as to what they ought to do for God.

The amount of work and service that is done for him in these United States in the way of church work and so on is enormous. An immense amount of human energy is expended in what is called serving God. I propose to consider briefly what serving God is and how a man may serve God best, and I think I shall be able to make plain that the conventional idea as to what constitutes service to God is all wrong.

When Moses went down into Egypt to bring out the Hebrews from bondage, his demand upon Pharaoh, in the name of the Deity, was, "Let the people go that they may serve me." He led them out into the wilderness and there instituted a new form of worship which has led many people to suppose that worship constitutes the service of God, although later God himself distinctly declared that he cared nothing for ceremonies, burned offerings, or oblation, and the teaching of Jesus, if rightly understood, would do away with organized temple worship altogether. God does not lack anything that men may do for him with their hands or bodies or voices. Saint Paul points out that man can do nothing for God, for God does not need anything.

The view of evolution which we have taken shows God seeking expression through man. Through all the successive ages in which his spirit has urged man up the height, God has gone on seeking expression. Every generation of men is more God-like than the preceding generation. Every generation of men demands more in the way of fine homes, pleasant surroundings, congenial work, rest, travel, and opportunity for study than the preceding generation.

I have heard some short-sighted economists argue that the working people of today ought surely to be fully contented because their condition is so much better than that of the working-man two hundred years ago who slept in a windowless but on a floor covered with rushes in company with his pigs. If that man had all that he was able to use for the living of all the life he knew how to live, he was perfectly content, and if he had lack he was not contented. The man of today has a comfortable home and very many things, indeed, that were unknown a short period back in the past, and if he has all that he can use for the living of all the life he can imagine he will be content. But he is not content. God has liked the race so far that any common man can picture a better and more desirable life than he is able to live under existing conditions.

And so long as this is true, so long as a man can think and clearly picture to himself a more desirable life, he will be discontented with the life he has to live and rightly so. That discontent is the Spirit of God urging men on to more desirable conditions. It is God who seeks expression in the race. "He works in us to will and to do."

The only service you can render God is to give expression to what he is trying to give the world, through you. The only service you can render God is to make the very most of yourself in order that God may live in you to the utmost of your possibilities. In a former work of this series[2] I refer to the little boy at the piano, the music in whose soul could not find expression through his untrained hands. This is a good illustration of the way the Spirit of God is over, about, around, and in all of us, seeking to do great things with us, so soon as we will train our hands and feet, our minds, brains, and bodies to do his service.

Your first duty to God, to yourself, and to the world is to make yourself as great a personality, in every way, as you possibly can. And that, it seems to me, disposes of the question of duty. There are one or two other things which might be disposed of in closing this chapter. I have written of opportunity in a preceding chapter. I have said, in a general way, that it is within the power of every man to become great, just as in *Science of Getting Rich* I declared that it is within the power of every man to become rich. But these sweeping generalizations need qualifying. There are men who have such materialistic minds that they are absolutely incapable of comprehending the philosophy set forth in these books.

There is a great mass of men and women who have lived and worked until they are practically incapable of thought along these lines: and they cannot receive the message. Something may be done for them by demonstration, that is, by living the life before them. But that is the only way they can be aroused.

2. The Science of Getting Rich

The world needs demonstration more than it needs teaching. For this mass of people our duty is to become as great in personality as possible in order that they may see and desire to do likewise. It is our duty to make ourselves great for their sakes, so that we may help prepare the world that the next generation shall have better conditions for thought.

One other point; I am frequently written to by people who wish to make something of themselves and to move out into the world, but who are hampered by home ties, having others more or less dependent upon them, whom they fear would suffer if left alone. In general I advise such people to move out fearlessly, and to make the most of themselves. If there is a loss at home it will be only temporary and apparent, for in a little while, if you follow the leading of Spirit, you will be able to take better care of your dependents than you have ever done before.

Chapter 21

A Mental Exercise

The purpose of mental exercises must not be misunderstood. There is no virtue in charms or formulated strings of words; there is no short cut to development by repeating prayers or incantations. A mental exercise is an exercise, not in repeating words, but in the thinking of certain thoughts. The phrases that we repeatedly hear become convictions, as Goethe says; and the thoughts that we repeatedly think become habitual, and make us what we are. The purpose in taking a mental exercise is that you may think certain thoughts repeatedly until you form a habit of thinking them: then they will be your thoughts all the time. Taken in the right way and with an understanding of their purpose, mental exercises are of great value; but taken as most people take them they are worse than useless.

The thoughts embodied in the following exercise are the ones you want to think. You should take the exercise once or twice daily, but you should think the thoughts continuously. That is, do not think them twice a day for a stated time and then forget them until it is time to take the exercise again. The exercise is to impress you with the material for continuous thought.

Take a time when you can have from twenty minutes to half an hour secure from interruption, and proceed first to make yourself physically comfortable. Lie at ease in a Morris chair, or on a couch, or in bed; it is best to lie flat on your back. If you have no other time, take the exercise on going to bed at night and before rising in the morning.

First let your attention travel over your body from the crown of your head to the soles of your feet, relaxing every muscle as you go.

Relax completely. And next, get physical and other ills off your mind. Let the attention pass down the spinal cord and out over the nerves to the extremities, and as you do so think: – "My nerves are in perfect order all over my body. They obey my will, and I have great nerve three." Next, bring your attention to the lungs and think: – "I am breathing deeply and quietly, and the air goes into every cell of my lungs, which are in perfect condition. My blood is purified and made clean." Next, to the heart: – "My heart is heating strongly and steadily, and my circulation is perfect, even to the extremities." Next, to the digestive system: – "My stomach and bowels perform their work perfectly. My food is digested and assimilated and my body rebuilt and nourished. My liver, kidneys, and bladder each perform their several functions without pain or strain.

I am perfectly well. My body is resting, my mind is quiet, and my soul is at peace.

"I have no anxiety about financial or other matters. God, who is within me, is also in all things I want, impelling them toward me: all that I want is already given to me. I have no anxiety about my health, for I am perfectly well. I have no worry or fear whatsoever.

"I rise above all temptation to moral evil. I cast out all greed, selfishness, and narrow personal ambition: I do not hold envy, malice, or enmity toward any living soul. I will follow no course of action which is not in accord with my highest ideals. I am right and I will do right."

VIEWPOINT

All is right with the world. It is perfect and advancing to completion. I will contemplate the facts of social, political, and industrial life only from this high viewpoint. Behold, it is all very good. I will see all human beings, all any acquaintances, friends, neighbors, and the members of my own household in the same way. They are all good. Nothing is wrong with the universe; nothing can be wrong but my own personal attitude, and henceforth I keep that right. My whole trust is in God.

CONSECRATION

I will obey my soul and be true to that within me which is highest. I will search within for the pure idea of right in all things, and when I find it I will express it in my outward life. I will abandon everything I have outgrown for the best I can think.

I will have the highest thoughts concerning all my relationships, and my manner and action shall express these thoughts. I surrender my body to be ruled by my mind; I yield my mind to the do minion of my soul, and I give my soul to the guidance of God.

IDENTIFICATION

There is but one substance and source, and of that I am made and with it I am one. It is my Father; I proceeded torch and came from it. My Father and I are one, and my Father is greater than I, and I do His will. I surrender myself to conscious unity with Pure Spirit; there is but one and that one is everywhere. I am one with the Eternal Consciousness.

IDEALIZATION

Form mental picture of yourself as you want to be, and at the greatest height your imagination can picture. Dwell upon this for some little time, holding the thought: "This is what I really am; it is a picture of my own soul. I am this now in soul, and I am becoming this in outward manifestation."

REALIZATION

I appropriate to myself the power to become what I want to be, and to do what I want to. I exercise creative energy; all the power there is, is mine. I will arise and go forth with power and perfect confidence; I will do mighty works in the strength of the Lord, my God. I will trust and not fear, for God is with me.

OTHER BOOKS YOU MAY LIKE

- 1984 by George Orwell, ISBN: 9789380914947
- 12 Years a Slave by Solomon Northup, ISBN: 9789390492374
- 51 Most Powerful Prayers by Ryan, ISBN: 9789354990847
- A Christmas Carol by Charles Dickens, ISBN: 9788193545874
- A Cloud by Day, a Fire by Night by AW Tozer, ISBN: 9789354990854
- A Passage to India by E.M. Forster, ISBN: 9789354990205
- A Room of One's Own by Virginia Woolf, ISBN: 9789354990281
- A Streetcar Named Desire by Tennessee Williams, ISBN: 9788194748601
- A Wrinkle in Time by Madeleine L'Engle, ISBN: 9789354991066
- Abraham Lincoln by Lord Charnwood, ISBN: 9789380914251
- Absolute Surrender by Andrew Murray, ISBN: 9789389716269
- Animal Farm by George Orwell, ISBN: 9789380914701
- Anthem by Ayn Rand, ISBN: 9789389157079
- As a Man Thinketh by James Allen, ISBN: 9788180320262
- As I Lay Dying by William Faulkner, ISBN: 9789390492381
- Awakened Imagination by Neville Goddard, ISBN: 9789389157086
- Be What You Wish by Neville Goddard, ISBN: 9789387669550
- Chanakya Neeti by Chanakya, ISBN: 9789389716276
- Civilization and Its Discontents by Sigmund Freud, ISBN: 9789387669499
- Delighting in God by AW Tozer, ISBN: 9788194748632
- Demian by Hermann Hesse, ISBN: 9789387669567
- Experiencing the Holy Spirit by Andrew Murray, ISBN: 9788194764809
- Feeling is the Secret by Neville Goddard, ISBN: 9789389157109
- George Orwell Combo : Animal Farm & 1984, ISBN: 9789390492459
- Gravity by George Gamow, ISBN: 9789388118484
- Guerrilla Warfare by Ernesto Che Guevara, ISBN: 9789354990366

Develop your reading habit | **Gift books to your friends**

OTHER BOOKS YOU MAY LIKE

- How to be filled with the Holy Spirit by AW Tozer, ISBN: 9789389157116
- How to Develop Self Confidence by Dale Carnegie, ISBN: 9789387669000
- In His Steps by Charles M. Sheldon, ISBN: 9789390492794
- Life of Christ by Fulton J. Sheen, ISBN: 9789389716306
- Lost Horizon by James Hilton, ISBN: 9789389716313
- Man: The Dwelling Place of God by AW Tozer, ISBN: 9789354990656
- Maneaters of Kumaon by Jim Corbett, ISBN: 9789354990731
- Mansarover 1 (Hindi) by Premchand, ISBN: 9789380914978
- Mansarover 2 (Hindi) by Premchand, ISBN: 9789380914985
- Meditation and Its Methods by Swami Vivekananda, ISBN: 9789389716320
- One, None and a Hundred Thousand by Luigi Pirandello, ISBN: 9789389716337
- Paths to Power by AW Tozer, ISBN: Forthcoming
- Scientific Healing Affirmations by P. Yogananda, ISBN: 9789389716344
- Selected Stories of Rabindranath Tagore by Tagore, ISBN: 9789380914770
- Siddhartha by Hermann Hesse, ISBN: 9789380914145
- Student's Encyclopedia of G. K. by GP Editors, ISBN: 9789380914190
- Tales from Shakespeare by Charles Lamb & Mary Lamb, ISBN: 9789380914367
- The Alchemy of Happiness by Al-Ghazzali, ISBN: 9789387669505
- The Book of Enoch by Enoch, ISBN: 9789390492480
- The Dynamic Laws of Prosperity by Catherine Ponder, ISBN: 9789388118156
- The Game of Life and How to Play It by Florence Shinn, ISBN: 9789387669390
- The Imitation of Christ by Thomas À Kempis, ISBN: 9789388118057
- The Knowledge of the Holy by AW Tozer, ISBN: 9789389157130
- The Law by Neville Goddard, ISBN: 9789390492886
- The Light of Asia by Sir Edwin Arnold, ISBN: 9789380914923
- The Magic of Believing by Claudie Bristol, ISBN: 9789388118149

OTHER BOOKS YOU MAY LIKE

- The Magic of Faith by Joseph Murphy, ISBN: 9789388118743
- The Miracles of Your Mind by Joseph Murphy, ISBN: 9788180320743
- The Mysterious Affair at Styles by Agatha Christie, ISBN: 9789390492510
- The Origin of Species by Charles Darwin, ISBN: 9788180320453
- The Plague by Albert Camus, ISBN: 9788194764892
- The Power of Awareness by Neville Goddard, ISBN: 9789387669406
- The Power of Positive Thinking by Norman Vincent Peale, ISBN: 9789388118569
- The Problem of Increasing Human Energy by Nikola Tesla, ISBN: 9789354990953
- The Prophet by Kahlil Gibran, ISBN: 9789380914022
- The Psychopathology of Everyday Life by Sigmund Freud, ISBN: 9789388118071
- The Pursuit of God by AW Tozer, ISBN: 9789389157147
- The Railway Children by E Nesbit, ISBN: 9789354990960
- The Red Badge of Courage by Stephen Crane, ISBN: 9789354990977
- The Sound and the Fury by William Faulkner, ISBN: 9789390492572
- The Stranger by Albert Camus, ISBN: 9789390492589
- The Sun Also Rises by Ernest Hemingway, ISBN: 9789354990984
- The Yoga Sutras of Patanjali by Patanjali, ISBN: 9789389716351
- Their Eyes Were Watching God by Zora Neale Hurston, ISBN: 9788194764885
- Think and Grow Rich by Napoleon Hill, ISBN: 9788180320255
- Thought Vibration by William Walker Atkinson, ISBN: 9789389157154
- To the Lighthouse by Virginia Woolf, ISBN: 9789390492190
- Who were the Shudras by Dr B.R. Ambedkar, ISBN: 9789354991028
- World's Best Short Stories: Volume 1 by Various Authors, ISBN: 9789390492275
- Wuthering Heights by Emily Brontë, ISBN: 9788193545898
- Your Faith is Your Fortune by Neville Goddard, ISBN: 9789389157161
- Zen in the Art of Archery by Eugen Herrigel, ISBN: 9789354991059

Develop your reading habit | **Gift books to your friends**

www.ingramcontent.com/pod-product-compliance
Lightning Source LLC
LaVergne TN
LVHW021943220826
846092LV00010B/1212

* 9 7 8 9 3 5 4 9 9 3 8 8 6 *